icky sticky readers

Splendid Sea Creatures

Laaren Brown

SCHOLASTIC INC.

New York Toronto London Auckland
Sydney Mexico City New Delhi Hong Kong

Dear family ʌ of new readers,

and friends

Welcome to Icky Sticky Readers, part of the Scholastic Reader program. At Scholastic, we have taken over ninety years' worth of experience with teachers, parents, and children and put it into a program that is designed to match your child's interest and skills. Scholastic Readers are designed to support your child's efforts to learn how to read at every age and every stage.

LEVEL 1 READER
- Beginning Reader
- Preschool–Grade 1
- Sight words
- Words to sound out
- Simple sentences

LEVEL 2 READER
- Developing Reader
- Grades 1–2
- New vocabulary
- Longer sentences

LEVEL 3 READER
- Growing Reader
- Grades 1–3
- Reading for inspiration and information

For ideas about sharing books with your new reader, please visit www.scholastic.com.

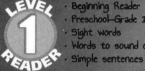

ICKY STICKY STICKERS

Every time you see this whale symbol, look for a sticker to fill the space!

> THIS BOOK IS TURTLE-LY COOL!

Contents

4 Splendid sea creatures

8 Sense and sound

12 Deep-sea defense

18 Dinnertime!

26 Meet the parents

28 Top 10 splendid sea creatures

30 Glossary

32 Index

ISBN 978-1-338-14416-1

10 9 8 7 6 5 4 3 2 1   17 18 19 20 21/0

Printed in the U.S.A.   40
First edition, April 2017

Book design by Penny Lamprell
Editorial by Hannah Wilson

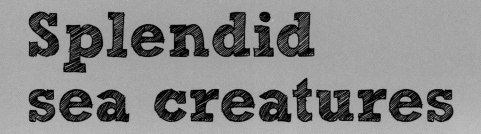

Splendid
sea creatures

Ready to dive deep into the world's oceans?
Want to see fabulous fish, scary sharks,
jiggly jellyfish, and oh-my-goodness octopuses?
One, two, three . . . jump in! Let's get wet
and wild with some SPLENDID sea creatures!

UH-OH, LET'S GO!
IT'S SCHOOLTIME!

4

SEA LION YOU LATER!

ICKY STICKY STICKERS

The clown triggerfish raises spiny fins to lock itself into a hiding place.

5

I'M A MAMMAL!

tail moves up and down

dolphin

Some sea creatures, such as dolphins and whales, are mammals, like us. They don't hatch from eggs. The females give birth to babies and feed them milk. Sea mammals swim to the surface to breathe air.

ICKY STICKY STICKERS

This beluga whale, like all whales and dolphins, breathes air through a blowhole on its head.

I'M A FISH!

gill flap

tail fin moves
side to side

Fish can breathe underwater. They have gills that
let them take oxygen from the water. Most fish
are covered with small, hard, thin scales that
protect their body. Gills plus scales equals FISH!

Sense and sound

In the vast oceans, sea creatures must hunt food, find a mate, and avoid bumping into things. But HOW? They use their senses! And sharks have superstar senses! They have great eyesight and can smell a drop of blood from far away. They can even sense electricity! With special parts on their snout, they detect the electricity given off by living things—like their dinner!

I SENSE DINNER.

NONSENSE!

When fish swim, their muscles produce electricity.

TOUCHY-FEELY

When narwhals tap tusks, they may be having a "chat."

Sea lions sense movements of prey with their whiskers.

Shrimp feel, smell, and taste with their antennae.

ICKY STICKY STICKERS

A loggerhead turtle may find its way by sensing Earth's magnetic field.

An octopus uses its suckers to taste new food.

HEARING is the number one sense for **humpback whales**. Male humpbacks love to sing, and they can hear one another's songs from hundreds of miles away! New songs usually start near Australia. Other humpbacks hear the tunes and start singing them, too.

CLICK

Dolphins have a special way to find prey using their hearing. It's called echolocation. They make clicking noises and listen to them bounce off fish.

Traveling from whale to whale, hit songs sweep across the Pacific Ocean toward California. WHY do the whales sing? Probably to impress the females!

QUIT WAILING!

Deep-sea defense

Sea creatures don't want to be MUNCHED for lunch. So they use all kinds of tricks to defend themselves. Some use mimicry (copying) to look like something bigger, stronger, or less tasty. The **mimic octopus** is one of the best copycats of all. This eight-armed wonder can change its looks to become a humble flounder, a venomous lionfish, or a slippery sea snake.

For a jet-like burst of speed, an octopus squirts water out of its body.

I MUSTACHE—HOW DO I LOOK?

DARING DISGUISES

flounder

Flounder? Nope—mimic octopus!

lionfish

Lionfish? Nope—mimic octopus!

sea snake

Sea snake? Nope—mimic octopus!

ICKY STICKY STICKERS
Looks like seaweed? It's really a leafy seadragon, a type of fish.

13

Camouflage is one cool defense. It means blending in with the surroundings—usually to hide from a predator. Meet a **cuttlefish**. This critter can change color SUPERFAST. Millions of sensors on its skin control little dots of color all over its body. Like a high-definition TV, it constantly changes its display to match the underwater world.

IF I CAN'T HIDE,
I INK AND SWIM!

SPOT THE CRITTER

HELLO? WHERE DID EVERYONE GO?

cuttlefish

Wobbegong shark

flounder

crocodile fish

ICKY STICKY STICKERS

A stonefish looks like coral. It has venomous spines that can kill.

A decorator crab wears tiny creatures for camouflage.

Not every sea creature hides. Some have WATERY WEAPONS for protection. Electric rays can zap a predator, while stingrays have venomous spines on their tails. The **porcupine fish** looks cute— until it feels threatened. Then it sucks in water, getting bigger . . . and BIGGER until . . . POP! Out come the spines!

CUTE?

GULP, GULP, GULP.

DANGER
220
volts!

venomous
spines

EEK!

An electric ray
makes electricity.

WHO'S CUTE NOW!

A stingray has venomous spines on its tail.

ICKY STICKY STICKERS
A hagfish, or slime eel, oozes snot-like slime to deter predators.

Dinnertime!

From the deep, dark depths to sunlit coral reefs, sea creatures must seek out dinner. Predators hunt other creatures, and they come in all shapes and sizes. The **peacock mantis shrimp**, no more than seven inches long, has the fastest animal punch on Earth!

BOO!

The shrimp preys on hermit crabs.

The shrimp strikes with front limbs like jackhammers, ripping and crushing to kill. You won't see this beastie in most aquariums—it can smash through glass! The shrimp lives in a coral reef, a colorful home for many fish and their food.

CORAL CAFE MENU

angelfish

sponge

fan worm

butterfly fish

parrot fish

coral

sardines

A thresher shark slaps prey with its tail.

BEHIND YOU!

Out in the open ocean, a **sailfish** hunts its prey with speed and style. The FASTEST fish of all, it easily catches up with a school of sardines. ZOOOOOM! Raising its sail to herd them, the sailfish pushes its long, sharp bill into the group. After some serious cutting and slashing, it's "so long, sardines" and "hello, fish fillets."

ORCA VERSUS SEA LION

1

2

3

An orca waits for . . .

. . . a sea lion!

Dinnertime!

top speed of sailfish:

68 mph

A great white shark snatches a seal with its razor-sharp teeth.

Blue whales, the largest creatures on Earth, eat tiny creatures called krill. With huge mouths gaping wide, they lunge at groups of krill, trapping them—and lots of water—in their mouths.

say it

krill

(say *kril*)
Small, shrimp-like ocean creatures.

New word

human: **6 feet**

When the whales close their mouths, the water is expelled, but the krill are trapped by special plates. Filter feeding in this way, blue whales can eat about six tons of krill in one day!

ICKY STICKY STICKERS
The largest fish is the whale shark, another filter-feeder.

blue whale: 107 feet

minke whale: 33 feet

Way down near the bottom
of the deep, deep ocean,
where the light of the Sun
cannot reach, there are some
very hungry sea creatures. But
HOW do they find food in the dark?
Some, like the giant squid, have HUGE EYES to
collect as much light as possible. Others glow,
lighting their own way. Anglerfish lure their
victims with built-in fishing rods.

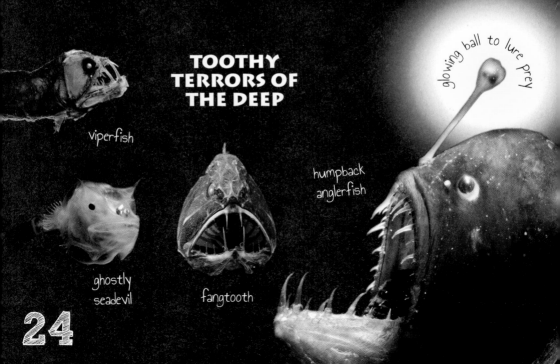

**TOOTHY
TERRORS OF
THE DEEP**

viperfish

glowing ball to lure prey

humpback
anglerfish

ghostly
seadevil

fangtooth

giant squid! **43 feet**

BIG AND BAD

Giant squid seize smaller squid with two long feeding tentacles.

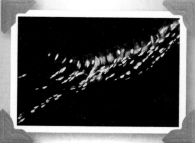

A siphonophore is a string of tiny creatures that can stretch for 100 feet! It glows to lure prey.

Jellyfish sting prey with their tentacles.

say it
anglerfish
(say *ANG-ler-fish*)
A fish that lures prey to its mouth with a body part that looks like a fishing rod.
New word

Meet the parents

Under the sea, many babies hatch out of eggs and swim away. They never meet their parents! But a baby **manatee** stays close to Mom for months. A manatee is a mammal. The baby is called a calf.

manatee calf

ICKY STICKY STICKERS

A baby walrus keeps safe with a piggyback ride from Mom.

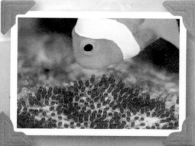

A clownfish tends to its eggs—
but it won't care for the babies.

For a **seahorse**, a type of fish, family life is all about the male. The female seahorse lays eggs in his pouch. The male keeps the eggs safe, supplying food and oxygen. After several days or weeks, he gives birth to baby . . . after baby . . . after baby— possibly up to 1,000 babies!

Baby seahorses emerge from the male's pouch.

MY BABY! ALL GROWN UP!

SAND TO SEA

1

A loggerhead turtle lays eggs on a beach.

2

About two months later, the babies hatch . . .

3

. . . and head to the sea.

TOP 10 splendid sea creatures

We've met some AMAZING ocean animals! Speedy fish, giant mammals, fearsome predators, and prey with perfect protection. But which of these cool critters are the most SPLENDID?

1 blue whale

IT'S AN HONOR. GOT ANY KRILL?

ME? REALLY? YAY!

dolphin

BACK OFF, BUDDY.

peacock mantis shrimp

ICKY STICKY STICKERS
Colorful Christmas tree worms look like . . . guess what?

Runners-up

4

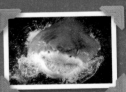

mimic octopus

5

great white shark

6

loggerhead turtle

7

cuttlefish

8

sailfish

9

leafy seadragon

10

porcupine fish

Glossary

anglerfish
A fish with a body part on its head that looks like a fishing rod. It lures prey to the fish's mouth and may have a glowing tip.

antenna
A long, thin body part on the head of an insect or sea creatures such as shrimp. This "feeler" is used for sensing.

bill
The long, narrow, bony upper jaw of fish like sailfish and swordfish. (The beak of a bird is also called a bill.)

blowhole
The breathing hole on the top of a whale or dolphin's head. It closes underwater.

coral
A tiny, blobby sea animal that lives in groups attached to rocks.

defense
Keeping safe from harm.

echolocation
A way that an animal can find food and other objects. The animal makes sounds that echo from (bounce off) the objects back to the animal.

filter feeding
A way of eating in which an animal takes in water, collects the tiny creatures living in it, and pushes the water out again.

gill
A fish's body part that gets oxygen from water. The water leaves the fish through an opening called a gill flap.

krill
Small, shrimp-like sea animals. Krill have antennae and 10 legs for swimming. Most are less than one inch long.

UH-OH, I'M FALLLLING . . .

magnetic field

The pushing away or pulling together power of magnets. Earth is a giant magnet. Turtles and some birds sense Earth's magnetic field and this may help them find their way during long journeys.

mammal

An animal that does not lay eggs but gives birth to babies. It makes milk to feed them. A mammal breathes air.

mate

A partner to have babies with.

oxygen

Found in air and water, oxygen is needed by animals to live.

predator

An animal that hunts and eats other animals.

prey

An animal hunted and eaten by other animals.

reef

A strip of rock, sand, or coral just below the water's surface.

school

A group of fish that moves together.

senses

Ways to find out about the world, such as seeing, hearing, smelling, tasting, and touching.

sensor

A body part on an animal that can help it find or notice something.

sucker

A cup-shaped body part. An octopus has suckers on its arms to grasp prey and pull itself along.

tentacle

A long flexible body part for grasping or sensing.

venomous

Poisonous and likely to cause harm.

TOLD YOU.

Index

A
anglerfish 24, 25

B
babies 6, 26–27
beluga whale 6
blue whale 22–23, 28

C
camouflage 14–15
Christmas tree worm 29
clown triggerfish 5
clownfish 19, 29
coral-reef fish 18–19
crocodile fish 15
cuttlefish 14, 15, 29

D
decorator crab 15
deep-sea fish 24–25
dolphin 6, 10, 29

E
echolocation 10, 11
electric ray 16

F
filter feeding 22–23
flounder 12, 13, 15

G
giant squid 24, 25
gills 7
great white shark 21, 29

H I
hagfish (slime eel) 17
hermit crab 18
humpback whale 10–11

J
jellyfish 25

K
krill 22–23

L
leafy seadragon 13, 29
lionfish 12, 13
loggerhead turtle 9, 27, 29

M
mammal 6, 26
manatee 26
mimic octopus 12–13, 29
minke whale 23

N
narwhal 9

O
octopus senses 9
orca 21

P Q R
peacock mantis shrimp 18–19, 29
porcupine fish 16–17, 29

S
sailfish 20–21, 29
sea lion 5, 9, 21
sea snake 12, 13
seahorse 27
shark senses 8
siphonophore 25
stingray 16, 17
stonefish 15

T U V
thresher shark 20

W X Y Z
walrus 26
whale shark 23

Image credits

WHO JUMPS NEXT?

LET'S FLIPPER COIN.

Can you find the right sticker for each page?
Read the sea creature's name, then find
the page with that name on it. Use the
extra stickers wherever you like!

clownfish

hagfish

beluga whale

clown triggerfish

baby walrus

whale shark

stonefish

leafy seadragon

loggerhead turtle

great white shark

Christmas tree worms